Did Y

SUF

A MISCELLANY

Compiled by Julia Skinner

With particular reference to the work of Clive Paine, Ian Robb,
Clive Tully and Carol Twinch

THE FRANCIS FRITH COLLECTION

www.francisfrith.com

First published in the United Kingdom in 2010 by The Francis Frith Collection®

This edition published in 2014
ISBN 978-1-84589-825-0

Text and Design copyright The Francis Frith Collection®
Photographs copyright The Francis Frith Collection® except where indicated.

The Frith® photographs and the Frith® logo are reproduced under licence from
Heritage Photographic Resources Ltd, the owners of the Frith® archive and trademarks.
'The Francis Frith Collection', 'Francis Frith' and 'Frith' are registered trademarks of
Heritage Photographic Resources Ltd.

All rights reserved. No photograph in this publication may be sold to a third party other than in the original
form of this publication, or framed for sale to a third party. No parts of this publication may be reproduced,
stored in a retrieval system, or transmitted, in any form, or by any means, electronic, mechanical, photocopying,
recording or otherwise, without the prior permission of the publishers and copyright holder.

British Library Cataloguing in Publication Data

Did You Know? Suffolk - A Miscellany
Compiled by Julia Skinner
With particular reference to the work of Clive Paine, Ian Robb, Clive Tully and Carol Twinch

The Francis Frith Collection
6 Oakley Business Park,
Wylye Road, Dinton,
Wiltshire SP3 5EU
Tel: +44 (0) 1722 716 376
Email: info@francisfrith.co.uk
www.francisfrith.com

Printed and bound in England

Front Cover: **IPSWICH, BUTTERMARKET 1893** 32204p
Frontispiece: **WOODBRIDGE, THE RIVER BANK 1898** 42772

The colour-tinting is for illustrative purposes only, and is not intended to be historically accurate

AS WITH ANY HISTORICAL DATABASE, THE FRANCIS FRITH ARCHIVE IS CONSTANTLY BEING
CORRECTED AND IMPROVED, AND THE PUBLISHERS WOULD WELCOME INFORMATION ON
OMISSIONS OR INACCURACIES

CONTENTS

INTRODUCTION

With Norfolk to the north, Essex to the south, and Cambridgeshire to the west, Suffolk occupies the middle part of that distinctive bulge in the east coast of Britain. The boundaries are fairly straightforward, topographically speaking. To the north, the boundary is the Rivers Waveney and Little Ouse, to the south the River Stour, while in the west it is largely where the more rolling Suffolk countryside meets the flat fens of Cambridgeshire. In the medieval period, Suffolk was divided into three areas. The Liberty of St Edmund was centred on Bury St Edmunds, and the Liberty of St Etheldreda on Woodbridge; the area between, called the Geldable, was administered from Beccles and Ipswich. In 1889 Suffolk became two counties: the Liberty of St Edmund became West Suffolk, and the other two areas became East Suffolk. This division lasted until 1974 when, under the Local Government Act, Ipswich became the 'capital' of Suffolk, although Bury St Edmunds retained its role as an administrative centre.

To many people, Suffolk might bring to mind the characterful, colour-washed timber-framed houses of places like Lavenham or Kersey, or the soaring splendour of its churches. To others, it might be that unique quality of light found on the coast at places like Southwold, and at Aldeburgh, which so inspired the Lowestoft-born composer Benjamin Britten. Along the coast, Walberswick proved a magnet to a whole host of distinguished artists, such as Charles Rennie Mackintosh and Stanley Spencer. Suffolk has some fifty miles of coastline, much of it with beautiful heaths as its hinterland. Over the centuries the shape of the coastline has changed considerably. Towns such as Aldeburgh, Dunwich and Covehithe have all suffered from erosion. It is hard to imagine that the tiny hamlet that remains of Dunwich is but a tiny part of what was once one of the country's major ports – the rest now lies beneath the waves. Elsewhere, the coastline has built up: Orford, for example, was once open to the sea,

and is now separated from it by a long spit of shingle that formed due to a process called longshore drift. Generally, the fact that Suffolk's coastline is all low-lying has put it at risk from tidal surges, the worst being the 1953 floods that affected much of the East Coast.

Along Suffolk's coastline a number of towns and villages became popular seaside resorts in the 19th century such as Southwold, Aldeburgh, Lowestoft and Felixstowe, and have remained so ever since. Lowestoft was described in 1886 as 'the very pink of propriety'. Felixstowe, following the visit of the German Empress in 1891, became known as 'The Queen of the East Coast Resorts'.

SOUTHWOLD, FROM THE PIER 1906 56829

SUFFOLK DIALECT
WORDS AND PHRASES

'Airy-wiggle' – an earwig.

'Holstes' – trousers that are too short.

'Lummox' – a clumsy person.

'Coupla three' – two or three.

'Arter' – after.

'Biddy' – an old woman, or a widow.

'Dwile' – cloth (from the Dutch word 'dweil').

'Shew' – showed.

'Mawther' – a young girl.

'Wholly' – very.

'Tye' – an area of common pasture, or a green.

'Rabbitin on like the brook' – talking too much.

'It's on the 'huh' – it's not straight.

HAUNTED SUFFOLK

There are many ghost stories around Suffolk. Here are just a few:

Gippeswyk Hall at Ipswich is said to be haunted by a White Lady who has been seen in the upper part of the hall on nights of the full moon. Another haunted location in Ipswich is the Woolpack Inn in Tuddenham Road, where a clairvoyant who was called in to investigate reported seeing a hunched grey figure disappearing into the wall of one of the bedrooms; later research found that the bedroom is next to a priest-hole, where Roman Catholic priests would hide during the days of persecution in the 16th century. Other ghosts said to haunt the inn are that of a pony-tailed sailor, an ex-landlord called George, and the shade of Admiral Vernon, who was MP for Ipswich from 1741 to 1754.

One of the most famous ghosts of Bury St Edmunds is the Grey Lady, the shade of Maude Carew who is said to have assassinated the Duke of Gloucester in 1447 at St Saviour's Hospital. Legend says that Maude killed the duke with a lethal poison, but then spilt some on herself and also expired. She was found by a monk as she lay dying and confessed what she had done; horrified, the monk cursed her spirit to roam for all eternity. Maude's spirit is said to return at precisely 11 o'clock on the anniversary of her death, 24th February, but to the frustration of ghost watchers she appears in different places throughout the town.

A ghostly man in tattered brown clothes is said to haunt the grounds of Roos Hall near Beccles. Reported sightings describe him gliding towards an old oak tree, and then vanishing away. Local legend says that he is the shade of a man who was hanged from the tree for theft, but evidence came to light after his death that proved his innocence.

The timber-framed Bull Hotel at Long Melford dates from c1450, and has been an inn since at least 1580. It is said to be haunted by the ghost of a yeoman who was murdered there in the 17th century.

SUFFOLK MISCELLANY

Henry II's great 12th-century castle stands sentinel over Orford. It was the first to be built with a keep that is cylindrical inside and polygonal outside, reinforced by three projecting rectangular turrets.

In medieval times, the most important industry in Suffolk was the wool and cloth-weaving trade, with various local variations of heavy broadcloth (the best-known came from Kersey) exported all over Europe. Large numbers of Dutch and Flemish weavers came to work and settle in Suffolk, helping to develop the county's important cloth industry, and many buildings in Suffolk have a pronounced Dutch influence. By the reign of Elizabeth I, the heavy broadcloths produced in Suffolk were going out of fashion, replaced by lighter and more colourful fabrics. Some Suffolk textile towns managed to adapt to the changing circumstances – Sudbury, for instance, became a centre for the production of fine silks.

ORFORD
THE CASTLE
1937 88243

LOWESTOFT, DRIFTERS c1955 L105110

Suffolk had a thriving fishing industry in the past, and the herring trade in particular made the fortunes of several coastal towns, especially Lowestoft, which was estimated to have 312 drifters and 139 trawlers in the 1880s. After a fishing trip, the drifters unloaded their haul into specially made wicker baskets for herrings known as 'swills', which were unique to Lowestoft and Great Yarmouth. Herring fishery in Lowestoft lasted until the 1960s, when the herring shoals had all but disappeared, the victims of over-fishing. Although Lowestoft's fishing boat numbers went into four digits, they never went beyond LT1299. This was because the number 13 is considered unlucky, therefore there was no registration LT1300 onwards. As numbers became vacant, they were re-used as needed.

Lowestoft is famous for its ancient thoroughfares known as 'Scores'. The name refers to paths or tracks which were literally 'scored', or cut, into the cliff face, probably in medieval times.

In the 18th century, one of Lowestoft's successful companies was Walker and Company – the Lowestoft China Factory. This made an immense variety of wares and was the first factory to produce seaside souvenirs – the famous 'Trifles'. A collection of Lowestoft China can be seen at the Lowestoft Museum in Nicholas Everitt Park.

Lowestoft as we know it today is the result of the vision of Sir Samuel Morton Peto, a successful builder and railway entrepreneur. In the mid 1840s Peto bought the sand-duned waste of Kirkley Heath where he built a new seaside health resort, serviced by a 'new town' that became Victorian Lowestoft. The centrepiece of Peto's 'new town' was Wellington Terrace, which was separated from Marine Parade by a mews enabling visitors to stable their horses and carriages for the duration of their stay. He also made improvements to the harbour, centred around a railway linking Lowestoft with Norwich, which helped develop Lowestoft's important port. He made a promise to local fishermen that he would deliver fresh Lowestoft fish to the markets at Manchester on the same day, resulting in the construction of a purpose-built fish market on the harbour's north pier, linked to the railway line.

**LOWESTOFT
THE SOUTH PIER
READING ROOM
1896** 37937

LOWESTOFT, LONDON ROAD SOUTH 1896 37925

One building that Victorian visitors to Lowestoft would have seen, but now lost to us, was St John's Church on the corner of London Road South and Belvedere Road, seen in photograph 37925 (above). St John's was built in 1854 but demolished in 1977, to be replaced by Levington House.

John Walter Brooke came to Lowestoft in 1874 and established his engineering works. By 1900, Brooke's had built up a considerable reputation for their marine engines, but between 1902 and 1914 the company also produced cars. A most unusual vehicle made by Brooke's of Lowestoft was the famous Swan car, built in 1910 for a wealthy eccentric Scottish engineer who lived in India. Complete with a carved head and body of a swan, it had a horn made of eight organ pipes. It is now in the Louwman national automobile museum at The Hague in the Netherlands.

The Britten Centre in Lowestoft is named after one of Britain's most famous composers, Benjamin Britten, born in Lowestoft in 1913. His father was a dentist in the town.

In the Middle Ages, Suffolk had such a large number of abbeys, priories, friaries and nunneries that it was known as 'Selig Suffolk', meaning 'Holy Suffolk'. One of pre-Reformation England's most important Benedictine abbeys was at Bury St Edmunds, which housed the shrine of St Edmund, the 9th-century Anglo-Saxon king of East Anglia who was killed by Danish raiders for refusing to renounce his Christian faith, and was later proclaimed a saint and martyr. The shrine of St Edmund became a popular place of pilgrimage, and the abbey of St Edmundsbury grew very rich and powerful – its abbot had jurisdiction over a huge area of Suffolk, as well as considerable legal powers over both the abbey and the town around it. Legend says that after St Edmund was killed by the Danes, his followers came to find his body and were led to his decapitated head by a great grey wolf – this is why a wolf guarding a crowned head features on the town crest of Bury St Edmunds.

In November 1214, under pretext of pilgrimage to the shrine of St Edmund, 25 barons of England secretly met at Bury St Edmunds and took an oath that they would compel King John to grant them their lawful rights and restore to the people their right to freedom from oppression. Some months later, at Runnymede in Surrey in June 1215, King John affixed his seal to the document now known as Magna Carta, or Great Charter. This is why the town motto of Bury St Edmunds is 'Shrine of a King, Cradle of the Law'.

In the Middle Ages, the tight hold of the powerful abbey at Bury St Edmunds over the town often led to disputes and conflict. In 1327 the abbot angered the townspeople by repudiating a new charter of liberties that he had agreed to, and over 3,000 rioters stormed the abbey, destroying the Abbey Gate and plundering the monastery. When the Abbey Gate was rebuilt, the new structure, seen in photograph B258501 (opposite), incorporated a guard room, a portcullis and arrow slits. Further violence against the abbey of St Edmundsbury occurred during the Peasants Revolt in 1381, when its prior was amongst those murdered by the mob that took over the town.

BURY ST EDMUNDS, THE ABBEY GATE c1900 B258501

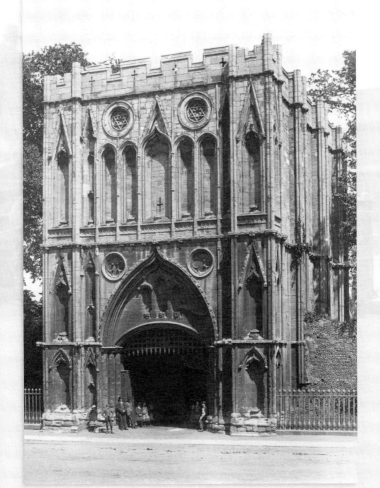

Hundreds of new homes were built around the abbey complex at
Bury St Edmunds in the 11th century, forming a medieval 'new town'
on a grid pattern devised by Abbot Baldwin in which Churchgate
Street was planned as the main thoroughfare, a ceremonial route
to St Edmund's shrine. The town was designed with an open space
opposite the main gate to the monastery complex – Angel Hill. For
the next 700 years this was the site of the town's markets and fairs,
including the famous 6-day-long Bury Fair, which made the town a
prosperous commercial centre of medieval England.

As well as having a considerable pilgrim traffic in the Middle Ages,
Bury St Edmunds grew into one of the leading cloth and agricultural
centres of the country. The importance of the broadcloth industry to
the town is recalled in the names of Looms Lane and Woolhall Street.

**BURY ST EDMUNDS
THE ANGEL HOTEL 1929**
81945

In medieval times, a white bull was kept close to the abbey at Bury St Edmunds in a meadow known as the Haberdon, for a ritual called the Oblation (or Offering) of the White Bull. The bull, decked with ribbons and floral garlands, was brought to the south gate of the monastery and led through the streets. Women who 'desired offspring' would walk alongside, with the monks and townspeople following in procession. The women then went to pray at the shrine of St Edmund and the bull returned to its meadow, the tenant of which held the land on condition that he kept a white bull in readiness.

In the early 12th century a church dedicated to St James was built within the abbey precinct at Bury St Edmunds. The abbey continued to grow and in the 15th century another church was built in its precinct, dedicated to St Mary. This church is noted for its decorated 'Angel Roof' and is also famous as the burial place of Mary Tudor, one of Henry VIII's sisters, whose story is commemorated in a window of the church. Briefly married to the King of France, after his death Mary married Charles Brandon, Duke of Suffolk and lived at Westhorpe. She died in 1533, and was buried in the abbey at Bury St Edmunds. After the abbey was closed down by Henry VIII in 1539, the king ordered that his sister's tomb be removed to St Mary's Church, where it remains.

St Wolstan's chapel in St Mary's Church in Bury St Edmunds contains the Suffolk War Memorial, and is now the Suffolk Regiment Chapel. The Suffolk Regiment, formerly the 12th Regiment of Foot, amalgamated with the Norfolks in 1959 to form the 1st Battalion of the East Anglian Regiment, which in 1964 became the Royal Anglian Regiment.

The abbey at Bury St Edmunds was closed by Henry VIII in 1539 as part of his dissolution of the religious houses. It is not known what happened to St Edmund's remains. The abbey lands were sold off and the abbey buildings fell into ruin, with much of the stone re-used elsewhere in the town, although the churches of St Mary and St James in the abbey precincts were spared, having been used by the townspeople for worship and guild meetings. The site of the abbey is now Abbey Gardens.

BURY ST EDMUNDS, THE FRINK SCULPTURE 2004 B258741

In the early 1900s there was a move for Suffolk to have its own bishopric. To reflect the east-west division of the county, it was decided that the new Anglican diocese would have the bishop's residence in Ipswich and its cathedral in Bury St Edmunds, and the Church of St James in the old abbey precinct was chosen to be the cathedral church for the Diocese of St Edmundsbury and Ipswich. The building was altered and extended in the 1960s, and a new east end was designed by the Cathedral Architect, Stephen Dykes Bower. The Cathedral Church of St James – St Edmundsbury Cathedral – has now also been given a handsome lantern tower, and in the Cathedral Close is a modern statue of St Edmund by Dame Elisabeth Frink.

In 1782 a young man from Norwich called Peter Gedge came to Bury St Edmunds and founded the town's first newspaper, the 'Bury and Norwich Post'. He is commemorated in a delightful epitaph on a tablet in St Mary's Church in the town, which reads:

> 'Peter Gedge, Printer, who first established the newspaper published in this town. Died January 7, 1818, aged 59 years. Like a worn-out type he is returned to the founder in hope of being recast in a better and more perfect mould.'

One of the historic buildings in Bury St Edmunds is Moyse's Hall. It was built around 1180, reputedly by a Jew called Moses, or Moyse, and its oldest parts are a fine example of the domestic architecture of the late Norman period. It has had many uses over the years, but was acquired by the Borough and opened as a museum in 1899. The museum's collection is diverse and ranges from rare Roman brooches to an exhibition of the work of Norah Lofts, the prolific historical novelist who lived at Northgate House in the town. One of the most gruesome items is a copy of the death bust of William Corder, who in 1828 was tried at the Shire Hall in Bury St Edmunds and found guilty of murdering his fiancée, Maria Marten, a crime that became famous as the Red Barn Murder. He was sentenced to be hanged and his body given to medical research. The hangman later had an account of the trial bound in leather made from Corder's skin, and this can also be seen in the museum.

BURY ST EDMUNDS, CORNHILL c1950 B258003

The handsome Market Cross building in Cornhill in Bury St Edmunds (the porticoed building seen in photograph B258003 above) was a refacing and enlargement of an existing building to a design by Robert Adam in 1774. In former times the ground floor was open and used as a corn exchange, and the upper floor was used as a theatre, which is why the exterior features a number of decorative theatrical masks and emblems. The building is now used as an art gallery.

The sugar beet factory outside Bury St Edmunds is the second largest beet factory in British Sugar. Its huge tower diffusers and five storage silos are a familiar sight from the A14. Bulk sugar is conveyed at the rate of 4,000 tonnes per week to the adjoining Silver Spoon packing complex for caster and granulated package production. The factory is supported by around 1,300 sugar beet growers in the area, and contributes an estimated £58 million a year to the local economy.

Many Suffolk villages and towns celebrated their prosperity from wool by building and decorating fine churches. The churches were decorated lavishly inside, with wall paintings illustrating religious themes, and brightly decorated rood screens were built across the naves of many churches. Much of this decoration was later destroyed or whitewashed over, as religious habits changed, but there are still some examples to be seen – for instance at Wenhaston, which has a famous Doom painting of c1500.

Holy Trinity Church in Blythburgh is one of the largest and grandest churches in Suffolk, known locally as 'the Cathedral of the Marshes'. The tower (which once had a spire) dates from c1330, but the rest of the church was rebuilt in the 15th century on a massive scale.

BLYTHBURGH, THE CHURCH OF THE HOLY TRINITY 1891 28357

A distinguishing characteristic of many Norfolk and Suffolk churches is a round tower, of which 38 survive in Suffolk. R327005 (below) of the church at Rickinghall shows an example of such a round tower, which has a 15th-century octagonal top with battlements. However, not all the towers are round as such – the tower of St Peter's Church at Gunton, Lowestoft, for example, is actually oval in shape.

Suffolk is famous for the medieval and Tudor timber-framed jettied houses and other buildings that can be found in many of its towns and villages. The early 16th-century timber building of Lavenham's Guildhall was commissioned by the Guild of Corpus Christi, a trade organisation that regulated the local industry of cloth production, and reflects the wealth of the wool trade. The building had a variety of later uses, including a jail, a workhouse and an almshouse.

RICKINGHALL, ST MARY'S CHURCH c1965 R327005

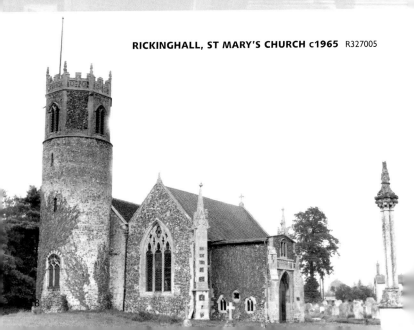

LAVENHAM, THE GUILDHALL 1904 51180

The spectacular church of St Peter and St Paul at Lavenham was rebuilt, except for the 14th-century chancel, between c1485 and 1525. Much of the money for the project was provided by the de Veres, Earls of Oxford and lords of the manor, and the Spring family, wealthy clothiers, and the exterior bears shields and heraldic devices of the two families to show which part they built. The porch, shown in photograph L21002 on page 47, is decorated with the de Vere stars, coats of arms and two boars – a play on words, as 'verres' is Latin for a boar pig.

The red-brick Tudor manor house of Kentwell Hall at Long Melford is notable for the striking Tudor Rose brickwork maze set into its courtyard. Also at Long Melford is Melford Hall, a fine Tudor turreted brick-built mansion that was originally used by the abbots of the Abbey of St Edmondsbury as a hunting lodge.

A landmark at Hadleigh is the Deanery Tower. When it was built in the latter part of the 15th century by Suffolk's Archdeacon William Pykenham it was planned to be the gateway to an ecclesiastical palace, but Pykenham's death put paid to further building. It is nevertheless a fine example of 15th-century brickwork.

In St George's churchyard at Shimpling, north of Long Melford, is a small building known as the Fainting House. In the 19th century ladies in the congregation would be taken there to recover if the combination of tightly laced corsets and lack of air became too much for them during a church service and they swooned.

LONG MELFORD, KENTWELL HALL 1895 35495

HADLEIGH, THE DEANERY TOWER 1922 71976

FELIXSTOWE, THE BEACH 1899 44516

A local landmark on the village green at Hartest is the Hartest Stone. This large glacial boulder was brought here from Somerton Hill in 1713 on a sledge pulled by forty-five horses to commemorate the Duke of Marlborough's victories in the War of Spanish Succession and the Treaty of Utrecht of 1713, which awarded Gibraltar to Britain.

In the 1870s the local landowner Colonel Tomline promoted a railway and a new dock at Felixstowe, in the hope of being able to compete with the port of Harwich across the Orwell Estuary. The dock did not succeed until well after his death, but the railway meantime stimulated the development of Felixstowe as a seaside resort. In the early years of the 20th century Felixstowe was at the height of its popularity as a seaside resort, with steamers pulling up at the pier with passengers from Great Yarmouth, Walton-on-the-Naze, Clacton, and even London. A popular form of entertainment for younger visitors was a ride in a cart pulled by a donkey, or perhaps a goat.

Sprats are caught by fishermen all along the East Anglian coast, but Aldeburgh and Southwold are particularly famous for these small fish, a small cousin of the herring. There was once a tradition that the first sprats of the season were sent from Aldeburgh to London for the Lord Mayor's Banquet.

On the beach at Aldeburgh are two curious old wooden towers. In the past, these were manned in stormy weather by two rival groups of local men, the Up-towners and the Down-towners, to watch for shipwrecks. If one was spotted, the two crews would race to get to there first, in order to claim salvage rights. The crews also manned the towers to pick up the lucrative pilot trade into the Thames estuary.

FELIXSTOWE, CHILDREN'S RIDES 1907 58978

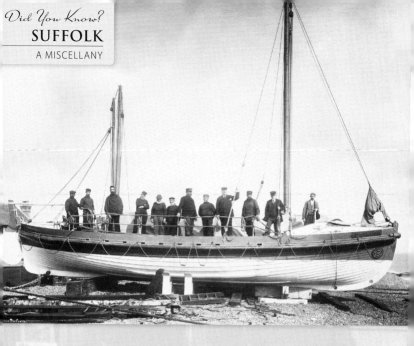

ALDEBURGH, THE LIFEBOAT 'THE CITY OF WINCHESTER' 1903 50426

Four years before photograph 50426 (above) was taken in 1903, an Aldeburgh lifeboat suffered its worst disaster, capsizing with the loss of seven lives; there is a memorial to the crewmen in the town. Here coxswain James Cable and his men proudly show off 'The City of Winchester', presented by that city as a replacement for the lifeboat so tragically lost a few years before. This boat served until 1928 and saved forty lives.

Aldeburgh was once the home of Elizabeth Garrett Anderson, the first woman Doctor of Medicine, and founder of a hospital in London. She became Mayor of Aldeburgh in 1908, which also made her the first woman mayor of an English borough.

When it was built c1540, the timber-framed Tudor Moot Hall at Aldeburgh was in the centre of the town's market place. Coastal erosion over the years has swept away much of the old town and now this historic building is on the seafront. The brickwork on the first floor dates from 1654, and so does the sundial on the end wall with the inscription 'I only count the sunny hours'.

ALDEBURGH, THE MOOT HALL 1896 38669

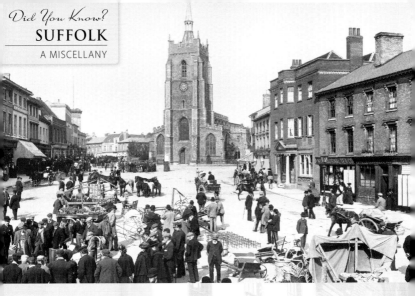

SUDBURY, THE MARKET 1904 51156

The famous 18th-century artist Thomas Gainsborough was born in Sudbury in 1727 and brought up in the town, and he lived in a house in Friars Street from 1748 to 1752, where two of his daughters were born. The house in which he was born stands in the street re-named to commemorate him, and is now a museum and exhibition gallery. It is the only artist's birthplace open to the public in the country. A statue of Thomas Gainsborough, palette in hand, now stands in front of St Peter's Church on Market Hill in Sudbury.

Inside St Gregory's Church in The Croft in Sudbury is a gruesome relic of the Peasants Revolt of 1381. Simon Tybald, 'Simon of Sudbury', was Archbishop of Canterbury and Chancellor of the Exchequer at the time of the Revolt, and was widely hated for imposing an unpopular Poll Tax. He was dragged out of the Tower of London where he had taken refuge and beheaded by the rebels. His head was taken back to his home town of Sudbury, where he had founded a college for priests, and his skull is now kept in the vestry of the church.

Suffolk's best-known painter is John Constable, born in East Bergholt in 1776. His father owned mills at Dedham and Flatford, and two windmills at East Bergholt and wanted him to follow in the family business, but John went to London to study art, eventually gaining a place at the Royal Academy. He painted the Suffolk countryside where he was brought up, working in a style which at the time was not generally popular. Constable's work only received recognition in Britain later on, but now his works are highly regarded. Flatford Mill, built in 1733, featured in several of Constable's works. Photograph 57554 (below) shows Willy Lott's Cottage beside the millpond at Flatford Mill, the setting for Constable's famous painting 'The Hay Wain'. Willy Lott, the mill-hand, is reputed to have lived in this cottage for eighty-eight years.

FLATFORD, WILLY LOTT'S COTTAGE 1907 57554

Most industries and crafts of Suffolk in the past were adjuncts to the two main spheres of agriculture and fishing. Agricultural machinery such as steam engines, steam and horse-drawn ploughs, seed drills and threshing machines was produced by Garrett's of Leiston, Smythe's of Peasenhall, Ransomes Sims & Jeffries of Ipswich, and Boby's of Bury St Edmunds – the latter firm gave its name to the 19th-century farming expression of 'Bobying' to describe the operation of cleaning straw and weeds from corn by means of a Robert Boby Patent Self-cleaning Corn Screening and Dressing Machine.

Suffolk contains some of the last great lowland heaths in Britain, sweeping down to reed-fringed creeks and extensive salt marshes which are the home of many rare birds. The Suffolk Coast and Heaths Area of Outstanding Natural Beauty (AONB) includes 35 miles of the Suffolk Heritage Coast and the RSPB's famous Minsmere reserve, where over 280 species of birds have been recorded.

SOUTHWOLD, THE LIGHTHOUSE 1891   28354

Looming over the rooftops of Southwold is the white tower of the lighthouse; opened in 1890, its light can be seen at sea up to 20 miles away. The strangely landlocked lighthouse was safely positioned away from the cliff edge but not too central to the town, where the smoke from coal fires might have obscured the light.

Southwold suffered a fire in 1659 which destroyed most of the town, but its 15th-century church of St Edmund survived. Inside the church is 'Southwold Jack', a rather menacing brightly-coloured warrior from the Wars of the Roses, whose duty is to strike a bell with his battle-axe upon the pulling of a cord, thus announcing the beginning of services. He will be familiar to drinkers of Adnams beer, brewed in Southwold, as he features on the Adnams logo. There is also a similar figure, known as 'Jack-o'-the-Clock', in Holy Trinity Church at Blythburgh.

The Sailor's Reading Room at Southwold was founded in 1864 by a naval widow whose intentions were 'to wean the fishermen from their alleged failings – going to sea on the Sabbath, and getting drunk on any day of the week'. It is now a fascinating place crammed with items of seafaring interest, such as paintings and photographs, model ships and memorabilia of the local fishermen, sailors and coastguards over the years.

Gun Hill at the southern end of Southwold takes its name from the six eighteen-pounder cannons that still stand there. They were presented to the town during the reign of George II (1727-60) after the local burghers had complained about its lack of defences, declaring that 'this place is in a very dangerous condition for want of guns and ammunition, being naked and exposed to the insults of the Common Enemys'.

DUNWICH, THE BEACH 1909 62044

Dunwich was once one of the most important ports in the country, but over the years coastal erosion and storm damage have taken their toll, and not much more than St James's Street is left of the town. When photograph 62044 (above) was taken, what remained of Dunwich still had the last of its old churches. The building, seen peeping over the cliff top in this view, finally fell into the sea in 1918.

Did You Know?
SUFFOLK
A MISCELLANY

The castle at Framlingham was built in 1190 by the powerful Bigod family, and was one of the first castles not to include a keep. Instead, it has thirteen separate towers, linked by a curtain wall, a Saracen idea brought back by returning Crusaders.

The font in the Church of St John the Baptist at Badingham features an item that is rather unexpected in a church. One of its carved panels shows a dying man being given the last rites by a priest, surrounded by his grieving family – with a chamber pot clearly shown beneath the bed.

FRAMLINGHAM, THE CASTLE 1909 62031

31

WOODBRIDGE, THE SHIRE HALL 1908 60685

The influence of Dutch architecture so common on the East Coast can be seen in Woodbridge's Shire Hall (photograph 60685, above). It was built in 1575 by Thomas Seckford, Elizabeth I's Master of the Rolls. The Dutch gables and double staircase leading to the upper rooms were added in the early 18th century. Woodbridge's most famous building is probably its old Tide Mill. Constructed in the 1790s, it remained in commercial operation until 1957, the last of its kind, using the tidal flow of the Deben for its power. The mill trapped water in the mill pond on the high tide, then operated for about two hours each low tide as the water was released. The Tide Mill was restored into working condition and opened to the public in 1972.

AN ARTIST'S IMPRESSION OF THE SUTTON HOO HELMET F6024

Sutton Hoo near Woodbridge was the site of the famous Anglo-Saxon ship burial that was excavated in 1939. No body was found in the remains of the ship, but recent research suggests there may have been a body there, which was destroyed by the acid soil. The ship was full of objects, or grave goods, many made of gold and silver, which are now on display in the British Museum, although there are replicas in Ipswich Museum. They included weapons, coins, armour and cups as well as garments and textiles, all of the finest craftsmanship, and the iconic helmet, made of gilded bronze. The opulence and value of these objects signifies a grave of someone of great importance, almost certainly a king. The dates of the coins found in the grave range between AD575 and AD620. Four major East Anglian kings are known to have ruled around this time – Raedwald, Eorpwald, Sigebert and Ecric – and Raedwald is thought to have been the most likely candidate.

An unusual feature of St Michael's Church at Beccles is that the 16th-century tower is separate from the nave, built this way because the slope of the ground meant the tower had to be built on firmer ground to the south-east of the main church building. In 1972 the town council bought the tower for the grand sum of one penny, which is preserved in a plaque in the wall, but then had to raise £68,000 to restore it. The tower now houses the photographic record of the Clowes printing works of Beccles, and other local information.

Bungay suffered a major town fire in 1688, and the Butter Cross was built to commemorate the disaster. It is a pretty octagonal building with a dome surmounted by a figure of Justice. In the past, a cage underneath the Butter Cross was used to hold local felons to public ridicule, although by the time photograph B617301 (below) was taken it was no longer in service!

The small town of Brandon in the Breckland area on the Norfolk/Suffolk border was once the centre of a flint-knapping industry; during the Napoleonic wars, it employed around 200 men producing gunflints.

BUNGAY, MARKET PLACE c1900 B617301

IPSWICH, ST PETER'S DOCK 1921 70411

Ipswich has been an important port for many centuries, situated where the River Gipping joins the head of the tidal Orwell estuary, but at the end of the 18th century large ships were no longer able to berth at its docks; the river was silting up, and even at high tide it was becoming impossible to get upstream. The revolutionary solution was to construct the Wet Dock in 1839-42 by isolating a bend in the river and diverting the river itself into a bypass channel known as the New Cut. With lock gates to control access to it, the Wet Dock provided the means for ships to be able to dock at any state of the tide and improved the facilities that Ipswich could offer. Today, Ipswich remains an important industrial and commercial centre.

In medieval times Ipswich created Port Men instead of town burgesses, because its wealth was dependent upon the river. This tradition is remembered today in the name of the town's football stadium, Portman Road.

IPSWICH, SILENT STREET, WOLSEY'S BIRTHPLACE c1955 I18047

On the corner in Ipswich where St Nicholas Street is joined by Silent Street stands a magnificent group of Tudor houses with a carved corner post (photograph I18047, above). Cardinal Wolsey, Henry VIII's powerful advisor and chancellor, was born in this area of the town in the 1470s, the son of an Ipswich butcher.

The Ipswich Transport Museum is unique in that it has the largest collection of transport items in Britain devoted to just one town. Everything in the museum was either made or used in and around Ipswich. The collection has been building up since about 1965, and moved to its current home in part of the former Priory Heath Trolleybus Depot in Cobham Road in 1988.

On the corner of Buttermarket with St Stephen's Lane in Ipswich is the Ancient House (or Sparrowe's House) with its incredible plasterwork – an interesting feature is St George slaying a dragon whilst wearing a top hat. Robert Sparrowe remodelled the building around 1670, with the pargetting (decorative plasterwork) reflecting his interest in the known world at that time – the plasterwork under each window represents Europe, Asia, Africa and America. Europe is depicted as an elegant lady with an open book; another lady under a palm tree is Asia; a naked man on a tree stump is Africa, and America is a nearly naked man in a feather headdress. The other major continent of the world, Australia, is missing – it had not been 'discovered' when the decoration was done in the 17th century.

From 1611 to 1634 Ipswich was a major centre for emigration to New England. This was organised by the Town Lecturer, Samuel Ward, whose brother Nathaniel Ward was the first minister of Ipswich in Massachusetts, USA.

IPSWICH, THE ANCIENT HOUSE 1921 70398

Four statues stand on the porch roof of the Post Office on Cornhill in Ipswich. They represent Industry, Electricity, Steam and Commerce.

Hidden beneath an Ipswich school playground is the Clifford Road Air Raid Shelter Museum. The air raid shelter was sealed up after the war and forgotten, but was discovered when workmen in 1989 found one of the entrances. The shelter was found to be in excellent condition, and in its new role provides a fascinating picture of life on the home front during the Second World War. Full of wartime memorabilia, the museum is open to visitors on certain days in the summer.

IPSWICH, THE POST OFFICE AND TOWN HALL 1893 32207

South of Ipswich is the redbrick Tudor folly of Freston Tower, seen in photograph 32233 on page 49. It is said to have been built by a wealthy Ipswich merchant, Thomas Gooding, around 1550 as a study for his daughter, Ellen, and she studied different subjects on each of its seven floors: on the ground floor she took lessons in the practice of charity; on the first floor she wove tapestries; on the second floor she studied music; on the third floor she studied ancient languages; on the fourth flour she read English literature; the fifth floor was her painting room; and the sixth, and highest room, was where she gazed at the night sky and studied astrology.

South of Ipswich at Tattingstone is a very curious building which is not at all what it seems. The 'Tattingstone Wonder' looks like a church, but is really a false front concealing a row of humble cottages behind it. It was constructed in the 18th century to give the local squire a more picturesque view from his manor.

The church of St John the Baptist at Needham Market was once a chapel of ease to nearby Barking. Inside the church is one of the most remarkable examples of a hammerbeam timber roof in East Anglia; built between 1458 and 1500, it has been described as 'the culminating achievement of the English carpenter'.

Stowmarket lies on the River Gipping, which in the 18th century was made navigable for shipping between Ipswich and Stowmarket by means of a series of locks and was known as the Ipswich and Stowmarket Navigation. Stowmarket's name means 'the principal place that holds a market' – the town was granted its market charter in 1347, and still continues to hold markets twice a week. Nowadays Stowmarket is the home of the Museum of East Anglian Life, sited behind the tourist information centre.

WOOLPIT, THE CARVED ROOF OF ST MARY'S CHURCH c1955 W442011

There was once a pit at Woolpit to trap wolves, and the original name of the village was Wolf Pit. St Mary's Church in Woolpit has an outstanding example of a double hammerbeam roof, an exclusively East Anglian structure of which Suffolk has two-thirds of the total (see photograph W442011, opposite). There are 106 angels on the hammers, wall plate and wall posts, all with outstretched wings hovering over the congregation at worship.

East Bergholt is famous for the unusual belfry of its parish church, which is a separate building, a bell cage, on the ground. The church was rebuilt in the late 15th century and the tower was started later, in 1525, but through lack of funds was never completed. The bell cage was probably erected as a temporary measure while the tower was built – but as that structure was never finished, it is still in use today. The bell cage is not unique in England, but the method of ringing the bells is. The bells are hung upside down and are swung by the ringer standing on the bell-frame, pushing the bells over by hand.

The 15th-century tower of St Mary's Church overlooks the market place of Mildenhall. The interior roof of the church has a particularly fine ceiling decorated with angels, bearing the marks of shots supposedly fired at them by Puritan soldiers during the Civil War. Mildenhall gained an airfield between the two world wars of the 20th century, which was the starting point for many famous air races. The airfield subsequently became a base for the United States Air Force (now the headquarters of the USAF in Europe).

The town of Newmarket was established c1200 as a 'new market' centre by Richard d'Argentien. During the Stuart era both James I and Charles II erected 'palaces' here as a result of their interest in horseracing in the area, and the aristocracy built their own residences during the late 17th and 18th centuries. The only part of Charles II's palace to survive today is incorporated into the 19th-century Palace House, in Palace Street, now the Tourist Information Centre. Further along Palace Street is the house that Charles II built for his mistress Nell Gwynne to use when she accompanied him to the town. Newmarket's real development occurred with the arrival of the railway in 1848, and many of the terraced houses built specifically for the railway workers still exist today.

The clock tower at the northern end of Newmarket's High Street was built to commemorate Queen Victoria's Golden Jubilee in 1887. Appropriately for Newmarket, the weathervane that tops the tower features a racehorse.

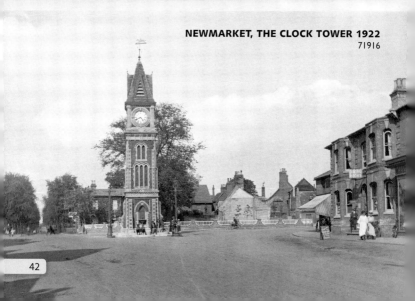

NEWMARKET, THE CLOCK TOWER 1922
71916

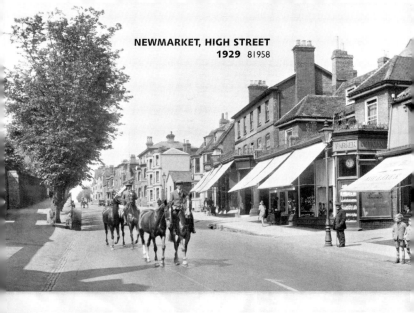

NEWMARKET, HIGH STREET
1929 81958

Newmarket has a local delicacy, the Newmarket Sausage, but two companies in the town make it and there is much rivalry over which is the true version; however, both are excellent. Although there are several different flavours, the sausages made by Musk's are made by mixing the meat filling with fresh bread, whilst Powters use the more traditional rusk; both companies use a closely-guarded secret spice mix in their products.

The Downs which enclose Newmarket are very suitable for horses – the underlying chalk ensures good drainage, and the flat land of the area is ideal for galloping – and have made the name of the town not only synonymous with horseracing, but also the breeding, selling and training of thoroughbred racehorses. The National Stud is at Newmarket, as is Tattersalls, the famous bloodstock auctioneers where the big names in racing come to buy their horses. Most of the 50-plus training stables with in excess of 2,000 horses are situated in Newmarket itself, and there are special horse routes through the town so the horses can be taken out safely for training on the turf gallops on the surrounding Heath.

SPORTING SUFFOLK

Newmarket's development as a horseracing centre dates back to the Stuart kings. James I discovered the suitability of the area for racing and established race meetings there, and his son, Charles I, inaugurated the first cup race at Newmarket in 1634. Charles II continued the links between royalty and racing at Newmarket, moving his court there from London at the time of the race meetings and filling the town with fashionable society. However, it was during the reign of Queen Victoria that horse racing at Newmarekt received its biggest boost, promoted by her son Edward, Prince of Wales, later Edward VII. Newmarket has two racecourses situated on Newmarket Heath, the Rowley Mile and the July Course, separated by the Devil's Dyke, a 6th-century defensive earthwork. The race meetings take place from spring to autumn, and nine of the country's Group 1 flat races are held there. Two of the five Classic races take place on the Rowley Mile Racecourse, the 1,000 Guineas for 3-year-old fillies and the 2,000 Guineas for 3-year-old colts and fillies but excluding geldings.

Ipswich Town maintain a fierce rivalry with their East Anglian neighbour Norwich City. When the two clubs meet, the occasion is called the 'the East Anglian Derby', but it is also known as 'The Old Farm Derby', a joking reference to the famous 'Old Firm Derby' played between Celtic and Rangers in Scotland. Sir Alf Ramsay, the manager who took England to World Cup victory in 1966, was also a one-time manager of Ipswich Town. Sir Alf lived and died in Ipswich, and a statue of him stands opposite Ipswich Town's stadium, Portman Road.

Speedway has a long and proud tradition in Ipswich, dating back to the very first meeting at Portman Road in 1950, and covering two incarnations of the Foxhall Stadium. The Witches' finest year though was surely 1998. The team won the Elite League by a massive 17 points, as well as the Knockout Cup and the Craven Shield. The strength of the team was such that three riders won individual championships, Tony Rickardsson (the World Championship), Chris Louis (the British Championship) and Scott Nicholls (the British under-21 title). Another Suffolk speedway team is the Mildenhall Fen Tigers, founded in 1975.

Felixstowe Ferry Golf Club is amongst the oldest in the UK, having been formed in 1880 - at that time the club subscription cost 5 shillings (25p!). Golf had been popular in Scotland for some time before this, but Felixstowe's was only the fifth golf club to be formed in England. A famous former captain of the golf club was the Rt Hon Arthur Balfour, who became captain in 1889 and was Britain's Prime Minister from 1902–1905. His love of golf is quoted on the club's website: 'My ideal in life is to read a lot, write a little, play plenty of golf, and have nothing to worry about'. According to 'Golf World' magazine, the course at Felixstowe is among the top 200 courses in the UK.

The first county cricket match was in 1764, when Suffolk played Norfolk at Bury St Edmunds Race Course (Norfolk won!). The present Suffolk County Cricket Club was founded in 1932 and plays home games at a variety of venues – Bury St Edmunds, Mildenhall, Ipswich, Copdock, Exning and Framlingham. The club plays in the Eastern Division of the Minor Counties Championship and has won the championship three times outright, in 1946, 1977 and 1979, and shared it with Cheshire in 2005.

NEWMARKET, RACEHORSES EXERCISING c1955 N23033

QUIZ QUESTIONS

Answers on page 52.

1. The smallest pub in Britain can be found in Suffolk. Where is it?

2. 'Thape' is an old Suffolk word for what sort of fruit?

3. One of Newmarket's two racecourses is called the Rowley Mile. How did it get this name?

4. Whereabouts in Suffolk will you find 'The House in the Clouds', and what was its original purpose?

5. Since December 2004, Lowestoft has had a distinctive landmark, known as 'Gulliver'. What is it?

6. A feature of St Michael's Church at Framlingham is the magnificent tomb of Thomas Howard, 3rd Duke of Norfolk, who was one of the most ruthless and powerful men of Henry VIII's court. He was the uncle of two of Henry VIII's six wives – who were they?

7. Many of Suffolk's most famous inhabitants have come from the arts – poets, painters or musicians. George Crabbe is probably the county's most distinguished poet, born in Aldeburgh in 1754. His poem about an embittered local fisherman inspired an opera by a much later and better known Suffolk man, Benjamin Britten. What was the fisherman's name, which is also the name of the opera?

8. How did Silent Street in Ipswich get its name?

9. Which historic vehicle run takes place in Suffolk each year?

10. What is the connection between Bury St Edmunds and an old speckled hen?

LAVENHAM, THE CHURCH PORCH c1955 L21002

RECIPE

GOD'S KITCHEL CAKE

It was a particular Suffolk custom for children to visit their godparents at Christmas time and ask for their blessings. A small cake called a God's kitchel was specially made for visiting godchildren. There was an old saying: 'Ask me a blessing and I will give you a kitchel', and in Chaucer's 'Canterbury Tales', written in 1386, we find the lines: 'Give us a bushel, wheat, malt or rye, A God's kitchel, or a trip of cheese.'

450g/1lb made-up flaky pastry
115g/4oz margarine
225g/8oz currants
25g/1oz sultanas
50g/2oz candied peel
75g/3oz sugar
50g/2oz ground almonds
1 teaspoonful powdered cinnamon
1 teaspoonful grated nutmeg

Melt the margarine in a large saucepan. Add the dried fruit, peel, sugar, ground almonds and spices. Mix well. Halve the pastry and roll one piece into a square about 30cm (12 inches) across – it should be rolled quite thin. Place it on a baking sheet. Moisten the edges of the rolled pastry with milk or water, and spread the filling on it, leaving an edge of about 1cm (half an inch). Cover with the second piece of pastry, rolled out to fit. Seal the edges well by pressing lightly together. Carefully mark the top of the cake with a knife into 6cm (2½ inch) squares, but without cutting through the pastry. Bake near the top of a pre-heated oven, 220°C/425°F/Gas Mark 7 until nicely golden brown.

Sprinkle with caster sugar and leave to cool for a few minutes, then divide into sections and leave them to cool on a wire rack.

FRESTON, THE TOWER 1893 32233

WALBERSWICK, THE FRUIT AND VEG STALL 1919 69128x

RECIPE

SUFFOLK APPLE CAKE

225g/8oz plain flour
1½ teaspoonfuls baking powder
A pinch of salt
115g/4oz lard or margarine
50g/2oz caster sugar
225g/8oz dessert apples (weighed after being
peeled and cored), either grated or finely chopped
A little milk

Pre-heat the oven to 190°C/375°F/Gas Mark 5.

Grease a baking sheet. Sift the flour, baking powder and salt into
a mixing basin. Rub in the lard or margarine until the mixture
resembles breadcrumbs, and stir in the sugar.

Add the grated or chopped apples to the other ingredients,
together with just enough milk to make a firm dough, and mix
well.

Flour your hands and form the dough into a round, flat cake
about 20cm (8inches) in diameter and about 1.5cm (¾ inch)
thick. Place the dough on the greased baking sheet and bake in
the pre-heated oven for about 45 minutes, until the cake is well-
risen and golden. Eat the cake hot, cut into wedges, split open
and spread with butter.

QUIZ ANSWERS

1. The 'Nutshell' pub in The Traverse in Bury St Edmunds is officially recorded in the 'Guinness Book of Records' as the smallest pub in Britain.

2. 'Thape' is an old Suffolk word for a gooseberry. Whit Sunday in May was traditionally celebrated in Suffolk with a gooseberry or 'thape' pie. Another fruity Suffolk fact is that the greengage, or green plum, is named after Sir William Gage, who lived at Hengrave Hall near Bury St Edmunds.

3. The Rowley Mile Racecourse was named after King Charles II, whose nickname of 'Old Rowley' was the name of his favourite racehorse.

4. When the seaside village of Thorpeness was first developed, there was no mains water supply. A five-storey house was built as a water tower, with a huge water tank on the top disguised with a pitched roof, chimneys and mock windows. The water tank has since been dismantled, but the unusual house remains, now used as a holiday cottage and known as 'The House in the Clouds'.

5. Towering over Lowestoft at Ness Point is 'Gulliver', the largest land-based wind turbine in the country. Constructed by SLP Energy, the turbine marks the start of Lowestoft's determination to be in the forefront of renewable energy.

6. Thomas Howard, 3rd Duke of Norfolk was the uncle of two of Henry VIII's six wives, Anne Boleyn and Catherine Howard. Despite the family connection, he presided over Anne Boleyn's trial on dubious charges of treason and adultery and passed the death sentence on her in 1536 so that King Henry could move on to his next wife.

7. Peter Grimes. The opera 'Peter Grimes' was one of the major works of Benjamin Britten, born in Lowestoft in 1913, who lived in the Red House at Aldeburgh from 1957 until his death in 1976 and was one of the founders of the Aldeburgh Music Festival.

8. All the inhabitants of the street died in the same outbreak of the plague, after which the street became sadly 'silent'.

9. The annual Ipswich to Felixstowe historic vehicle road run, which takes place every May. It is organised by the Ipswich Transport Museum and starts at Christchurch Park in Ipswich, finishing at the promenade in Felixstowe.

10. 'Old Speckled Hen' is one of the 'strong fine ales' produced by the Greene King brewery in Bury St Edmunds. Benjamin Greene founded the company in 1799 and passed it on to his son, Edward Greene, who went into partnership Frederick King.

THORPENESS, THE HOUSE IN THE CLOUDS c1955 T38004

FRANCIS FRITH

PIONEER VICTORIAN PHOTOGRAPHER

Francis Frith, founder of the world-famous photographic archive, was a complex and multi-talented man. A devout Quaker and a highly successful Victorian businessman, he was philosophical by nature and pioneering in outlook. By 1855 he had already established a wholesale grocery business in Liverpool, and sold it for the astonishing sum of £200,000, which is the equivalent today of over £15,000,000. Now in his thirties, and captivated by the new science of photography, Frith set out on a series of pioneering journeys up the Nile and to the Near East.

INTRIGUE AND EXPLORATION

He was the first photographer to venture beyond the sixth cataract of the Nile. Africa was still the mysterious 'Dark Continent', and Stanley and Livingstone's historic meeting was a decade into the future. The conditions for picture taking confound belief. He laboured for hours in his wicker dark-room in the sweltering heat of the desert, while the volatile chemicals fizzed dangerously in their trays. Back in London he exhibited his photographs and was 'rapturously cheered' by members of the Royal Society. His reputation as a photographer was made overnight.

VENTURE OF A LIFE-TIME

By the 1870s the railways had threaded their way across the country, and Bank Holidays and half-day Saturdays had been made obligatory by Act of Parliament. All of a sudden the working man and his family were able to enjoy days out, take holidays, and see a little more of the world.

With typical business acumen, Francis Frith foresaw that these new tourists would enjoy having souvenirs to commemorate their days out. For the next thirty years he travelled the country by train and by pony and trap, producing fine photographs of seaside resorts and beauty spots that were keenly bought by millions of Victorians. These prints were painstakingly pasted into family albums and pored over during the dark nights of winter, rekindling precious memories of summer excursions. Frith's studio was soon supplying retail shops all over the country, and by 1890 F Frith & Co had become the greatest specialist photographic publishing company in the world, with over 2,000 sales outlets, and pioneered the picture postcard.

FRANCIS FRITH'S LEGACY

Francis Frith had died in 1898 at his villa in Cannes, his great project still growing. By 1970 the archive he created contained over a third of a million pictures showing 7,000 British towns and villages.

Frith's legacy to us today is of immense significance and value, for the magnificent archive of evocative photographs he created provides a unique record of change in the cities, towns and villages throughout Britain over a century and more. Frith and his fellow studio photographers revisited locations many times down the years to update their views, compiling for us an enthralling and colourful pageant of British life and character.

We are fortunate that Frith was dedicated to recording the minutiae of everyday life. For it is this sheer wealth of visual data, the painstaking chronicle of changes in dress, transport, street layouts, buildings, housing and landscape that captivates us so much today, offering us a powerful link with the past and with the lives of our ancestors.

Computers have now made it possible for Frith's many thousands of images to be accessed almost instantly. The archive offers every one of us an opportunity to examine the places where we and our families have lived and worked down the years. Its images, depicting our shared past, are now bringing pleasure and enlightenment to millions around the world a century and more after his death.

For further information visit: www.francisfrith.com

INTERIOR DECORATION

Frith's photographs can be seen framed and as giant wall murals in thousands of pubs, restaurants, hotels, banks, retail stores and other public buildings throughout Britain. These provide interesting and attractive décor, generating strong local interest and acting as a powerful reminder of gentler days in our increasingly busy and frenetic world.

FRITH PRODUCTS

All Frith photographs are available as prints and posters in a variety of different sizes and styles. In the UK we also offer a range of other gift and stationery products illustrated with Frith photographs, although many of these are not available for delivery outside the UK – see our web site for more information on the products available for delivery in your country.

THE INTERNET

Over 100,000 photographs of Britain can be viewed and purchased on the Frith web site. The web site also includes memories and reminiscences contributed by our customers, who have personal knowledge of localities and of the people and properties depicted in Frith photographs. If you wish to learn more about a specific town or village you may find these reminiscences fascinating to browse. Why not add your own comments if you think they would be of interest to others? See **www.francisfrith.com**

PLEASE HELP US BRING FRITH'S PHOTOGRAPHS TO LIFE

Our authors do their best to recount the history of the places they write about. They give insights into how particular towns and villages developed, they describe the architecture of streets and buildings, and they discuss the lives of famous people who lived there. But however knowledgeable our authors are, the story they tell is necessarily incomplete.

Frith's photographs are so much more than plain historical documents. They are living proofs of the flow of human life down the generations. They show real people at real moments in history; and each of those people is the son or daughter of someone, the brother or sister, aunt or uncle, grandfather or grandmother of someone else. All of them lived, worked and played in the streets depicted in Frith's photographs.

We would be grateful if you would give us your insights into the places shown in our photographs: the streets and buildings, the shops, businesses and industries. Post your memories of life in those streets on the Frith website: what it was like growing up there, who ran the local shop and what shopping was like years ago; if your workplace is shown tell us about your working day and what the building is used for now. Read other visitors' memories and reconnect with your shared local history and heritage. With your help more and more Frith photographs can be brought to life, and vital memories preserved for posterity, and for the benefit of historians in the future.

Wherever possible, we will try to include some of your comments in future editions of our books. Moreover, if you spot errors in dates, titles or other facts, please let us know, because our archive records are not always completely accurate—they rely on 140 years of human endeavour and hand-compiled records. You can email us using the contact form on the website.

Thank you!

For further information, trade, or author enquiries
please contact us at the address below:

**The Francis Frith Collection, 6 Oakley Business Park,
Wylye Road, Dinton, Wiltshire SP3 5EU.**
Tel: +44 (0)1722 716 376 Fax: +44 (0)1722 716 881
e-mail: sales@francisfrith.co.uk **www.francisfrith.com**